Building Blocks

Diane Califano

American Quilter's Society
www.AmericanQuilter.com

The American Quilter's Society or AQS is dedicated to quilting excellence. AQS promotes the triumphs of today's quilter, while remaining dedicated to the quilting tradition. AQS believes in the promotion of this art and craft through AQS Publishing and AQS QuiltWeek®.

DIRECTOR OF PUBLICATIONS: KIMBERLY HOLLAND TETREV
COPY EDITOR: ADRIANA FITCH
PROOFREADER: GINA SCHADE
ILLUSTRATIONS: SARAH BOZONE
GRAPHIC DESIGN: SARAH BOZONE AND ELAINE WILSON
COVER DESIGN: MICHAEL BUCKINGHAM
QUILT PHOTOGRAPHY: CHARLES R. LYNCH

Additional copies of this book may be ordered from the American Quilter's Society, PO Box 3290, Paducah, KY 42002-3290, or online at www.ShopAQS.com.

Attention Photocopying Service: Please note the following—Publisher and author give permission to print pages 18, 42, 50, 54, 55, and 69.

Text © 2015, Author, Diane Califano
Artwork © 2015, American Quilter's Society

American Quilter's Society

www.AmericanQuilter.com

Library of Congress Cataloging-in-Publication Data

Names: Califano, Diane, author.
Title: Building blocks : back to quilt basics / By Diane Califano.
Description: Paducah, KY : American Quilter's Society, 2015.
Identifiers: LCCN 2015041955 (print) | LCCN 2015042658 (ebook) | ISBN
   9781604601435 (pbk.) | ISBN 9781604603095 (e-book)
Subjects: LCSH: Patchwork--Patterns. | Quilting--Patterns.
Classification: LCC TT835 .C354 2015 (print) | LCC TT835 (ebook) | DDC
   746.46--dc23
LC record available at http://lccn.loc.gov/2015041955

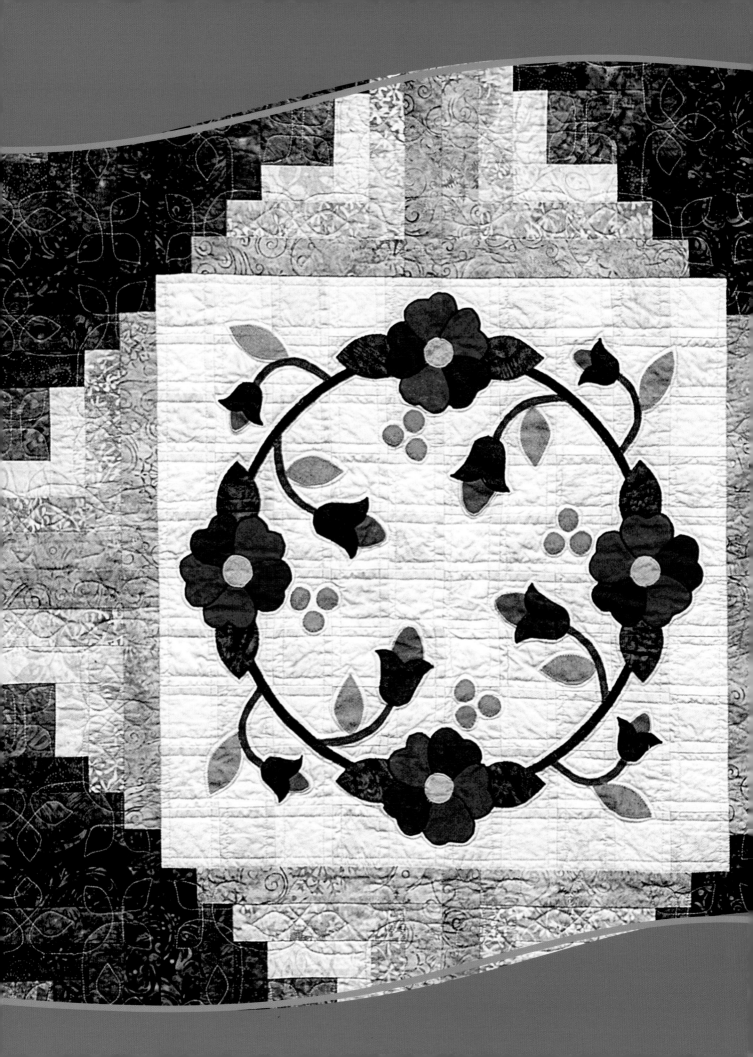

BUILDING BLOCKS, 100" x 100"
Designed and made by Diane Califano

Contents

Getting Started

Introduction

This project will teach a variety of machine quiltmaking techniques for all skill levels that can be applied to all styles of quilts. These techniques will be applied to the featured quilt and will cover the entire quiltmaking process, from fabric selection and piecing, to quilting and finishing.

The blocks for the featured quilt have been selected to showcase a variety of piecing methods that are commonly used in quilt patterns. By the end of this book, you will have the confidence to tackle any quilt pattern.

Work Space

A work space or sewing area involves several personal decisions. My preferences are to have my sewing machine on the right half of the table and my cutting mat on the left half of the table, as shown below. My ironing board is set up at table height on the left end of the table creating an "L" shape. I have a multiple-drawer cart on the right end of the table that accommodates all my accessories, such as pins, scissors, stitch ripper,

rotary cutter, etc. For efficiency, I like a chair with wheels so I can move from one station to the next without much effort. I also like a large cutting mat on the backside of the sewing machine for cutting larger pieces.

Needles

I prefer using a topstitch needle for almost all my sewing. It is a versatile needle with a sharp point that slides in and out of the fabric with very little friction. For sewing my block pieces together, I use a size 80/12 needle.

Needle Setting

When I am piecing, I like to stop sewing with the needle in the down position. This helps to hold the fabric in place as I make any needed adjustments to what I am sewing. If your machine has a setting to stop with the needle in the down position, it may also slightly lift the presser foot at the same time. This allows you to easily feed the next piece of fabric into the machine, which makes chain sewing easier.

Thread

I prefer a thin (50 wt.) but strong thread for almost all my sewing. A thread with a lot of bulk can decrease the accuracy of the piecing. The bulkier threads tend to produce more lint, which means more time spent cleaning the bobbin area. I like to match the type of thread to the type of fabric. For example, if I am sewing on cotton fabric, I use a cotton thread.

Seam Allowance

For the piecing, use a precise ¼" seam allowance, unless otherwise noted. An easy way to sew with a consistent seam allowance is to provide a guide on the throat plate for your fabric to move along. This can be done by marking the throat plate ¼" away from the needle. Blue painter's tape works great as it leaves very little sticky residue when removed. By stacking a few Post-it® notes at this location, you can create a ridge for your fabric to move along. A lot of machines have a ¼" piecing foot. Verify that the needle is ¼" away from the edge of the foot.

Seams

Notice that most of the seams are crossed with another seam. For this reason, there is no need to lock the beginning and ending of every seam.

Pressing the seam is very important. A smoother and more precise crease is created by pressing the seam before pressing out the seam allowance. Pressing a narrow seam allowance

to one side creates a stronger seam than if it were pressed open. Throughout this quilt, it is recommended the seam allowances be pressed to one side.

Finished Size vs. Cut Size

The term finished size refers to the size the piece or block will be within the quilt. The cut size refers to the size you cut the piece or the size the block will be as it stands alone, before it is pieced into the quilt.

Since a ¼" seam allowance will be used throughout, the finished size of any of the pieces or blocks will be ½" smaller than the cut size. The cut size includes the ¼" seam allowance on each side of the length and width of the piece or block.

Estimating Fabric Yardage

All cutting directions are based on a usable fabric width of 40". Most fabric comes in a width that varies from about 42" to 45". Once the selvage is removed, the fabric's usable width is reduced to no less than 40".

Value vs. Color

Most patterns will list how much of each fabric is needed to complete the project. Chances are, when fabric is selected, the exact fabric used in the pattern cannot be found. However, by understanding value and color, substitute fabrics can be easily found for the ones the pattern suggests.

We live in a world of color and are very influenced by it. We may see a quilt and like it, or not like it, simply because of the colors. When we make our own quilt, we can select whatever colors we desire. So the challenge is to select fabric with the same values as the pattern, not necessarily the same colors.

When it comes to value vs. color, think of a black-and-white picture vs. a color photo. The black-and-white photo shows only values of black and white. The color photo can show innumerable colors, but still shows the same value as the black-and-white picture, as shown below.

Consider the following quilt block. All of the blocks utilize the same pattern, but they look very different from each other just by changing the location of the values.

So, when selecting the fabric, pick colors you like that coordinate well together, but also make sure to select a range of values. The design of a quilt can be interpreted in many colors, but as long as the values are placed properly, the integrity of the design is maintained.

How do we distinguish value when we live in a world of color? One of the easiest ways is to make a black-and-white copy. By copying a pattern into a black-and-white picture, the value placement can easily be distinguished. Remember, consistent value placement will allow the design intent to be maintained.

Another way to view value without being influenced by color is to view fabrics through colored cellophane or glass. This will wash the color out so only the value will read. This is helpful for viewing fabric in a store, where copying into black and white is not feasible. When selecting fabric, I like to try to think in terms of light, medium, and dark, rather than specific colors.

Light	Medium	Dark

Within each of these values, I try to select two or three more fabrics to provide additional interest.

Light	Medium	Dark

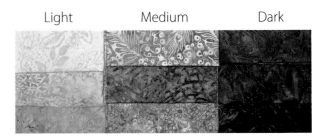

I often add a background color of fabric to provide contrast in the quilt. Depending on the fabric selection, I will usually choose white, off-white, or black.

After I select my fabric, I like to verify the values with a black-and-white photo or wash of color.

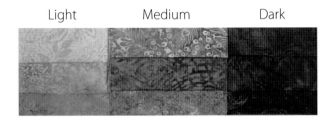

Light   Medium   Dark

Light   Medium   Dark

Now I can easily substitute my fabrics for the ones used in the pattern, simply by matching the values.

To Prewash or Not to Prewash

Once the fabric is selected decide about prewashing. By prewashing, you are preshrinking the fabric. This can help to eliminate distortion of a quilt during future washings. Prewashing will help set colors so they will not run onto other fabrics within a quilt during future washings. It also helps to eliminate factory chemicals.

I tend to prewash if I am using yardages of fabric. So that I don't end up with a big ball of knotted thread, I sew the raw edges of like-colored fabrics together before washing. This reduces fraying, knotting, and distortion of fabric through the wash and dry cycles.

I do not prewash if I am using precut fabric pieces, such as precut strips (jelly roll) or precut squares (charm packs and layer cakes).

I iron my fabric with starch before I start cutting. This helps to increase accuracy with both the cutting and piecing of the fabric since it is more stable and less likely to stretch.

Template and Strip Cutting

I find cutting the fabric almost as much fun as piecing it back together. Most quilt patterns are designed so the fabric can be cut with a template or strip cut.

To cut fabric using a template, use the template to trace the shape onto the wrong side of the fabric. Cut out the traced shapes with scissors. This method is particularly good for cutting odd, curved, or complicated shapes, or for fussy cutting (cutting a particular motif from the fabric pattern). Cutting using templates or patterns was very popular before the rotary cutter was invented.

With the rotary cutter, fabric can be strip cut. This method is fast because multiple layers can be cut at one time. The first step is to "square-up" the fabric, or find the straight of grain. This will give a straight edge to reference all the cuts. If the fabric edge is not squared up before strip cutting, the result will be a zigzag strip of fabric rather than a straight strip.

I have found the easiest way to square-up the fabric is to fold it selvage to selvage (the selvage is the manufactured finished edge of the fabric), hold it up, and slide the selvage edges along each other until the fabric hangs with no wrinkles.

Once the fabric is folded on the straight of grain, place it onto a cutting mat and bring the fold up to the selvages so there are four layers of fabric. Align an acrylic ruler along the folded edge of the fabric and near the raw edge. Butt another acrylic ruler so it covers the raw edge, then remove the acrylic ruler along the folded edge and cut the raw edge away to square the end of the fabric, as shown below.

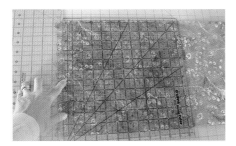

After the fabric is squared, continue cutting by aligning the acrylic ruler along the cut edge and fold at the desired increment and cut. As general rules, you always want your acrylic ruler covering up the strip you are cutting and want to move the rotary cutter away from you as you cut.

A slotted ruler is particularly helpful to square and cut fabric if you are cutting in ½" increments (or ¼", depending on the size of your slotted ruler). Simply align the bottom line of the slotted ruler with the fold of the fabric, cut away the raw edges, and continue cutting your fabric at the desired increment.

Fabric Requirements

Background Fabrics
2⅝ yards Background #1
2 yards Background #2
1½ yards Background #3

Light Fabrics
¼ yard Light #1
1⅝ yards Light #2
1 yard Light #3

Medium Fabrics
⅔ yard Medium #1
1⅜ yards Medium #2
1¼ yards Medium #3

Dark Fabrics
1⅓ yards Dark #1
1¼ yards Dark #2
1⅛ yards Dark #3

Other Fabric
1 yard for binding
9 yards for backing

Other Supplies
2 yards fusible feather weight interfacing
2 yards of iron-on adhesive paper*
104" square of batting
Quilt in a Day® Flying Geese Ruler
Sewing machine and related supplies
Rotary cutter and related supplies
*Quilter used ThermoWeb HeatnBond® Lite

Log Cabin Block

The Log Cabin block shown below is constructed using a strip-piecing technique. The blocks are made by sewing the fabric to the block and then cutting the piece to the proper size. This technique is often used to attach sashing, borders, and binding.

The Log Cabin block will teach these techniques:

- Cutting fabric accurately
- Sewing with a precise ¼" seam allowance
- Pressing seams
- Pressing seam allowances
- Making sure the seam allowance feeds through the machine in the direction it was pressed

Cutting Instructions

Light Fabric #1 – Cut (3) 1¾" width-of-fabric (WOF) strips.

Light Fabric #2 – Cut (5) 1¾" WOF strips.

Light Fabric #3 – Cut (6) 1¾" WOF strips.

Medium Fabric #1 – Cut (1) 3" WOF strip.

Dark Fabric #1 – Cut (4) 1¾" WOF strips.

Dark Fabric #2 – Cut (5) 1¾" WOF strips.

Dark Fabric #3 – Cut (6) 1¾" WOF strips.

The diagram below shows the values of the Log Cabin block in black and white. It is a gradation of light on one side and dark on the other side with a medium value in the center. The center is traditionally red, although not required.

Log Cabin Block
Make 12

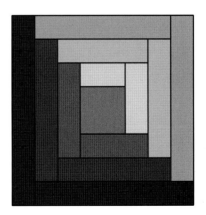

Assembling the Block

1. Stack strips in the following order:

Medium #1 (on top), Light #1, Dark #1, Light #2, Dark #2, Light #3, and Dark #3 (on the bottom).

2. Place the medium fabric strip right side up. Place the next strip in the stack, light fabric #1, on top of the medium strip with right sides together. Align the long edges on the right side. Sew the length of the strips.

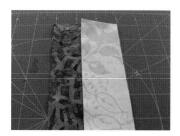

3. Cut the sewn unit into (12) 3" pieces.

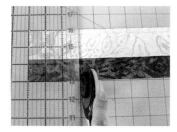

4. Place the units on the ironing board, with the light fabric facing up. Press the seam, then flip the top fabric right-side up and press the unit open.

5. Stack all 12 units right-side down. Turn each unit so the light fabric is oriented above the medium fabric.

6. Lay the next light fabric strip right-side up in front of the needle. Pick up a sewn unit as it was laid out and put it on top of the light fabric strip with right sides together, aligning the right side.

7. Sew to the end of the sewn unit, ensuring that the seam allowance is flat in the direction it was pressed. Add another sewn unit on top of the strip, right sides together, butting it to the end of the first sewn unit. Sew to the end of the sewn unit. Repeat until all 12 units are sewn to the light fabric #1 strips. If a strip will not accommodate a full unit, start another strip of the same fabric.

8. Trim the beginning and the ending of the tail of the fabric strip just sewn.

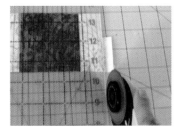

9. Cut the units apart where they butt up next to each other. Because the units were butted together for sewing, one cut will divide them evenly, leaving a trimmed straight edge.

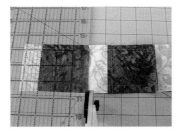

10. Place each of the 12 units on the ironing board with the piece just sewn facing up. Press the seam, then flip the top fabric right-side up and press the unit open.

11. Stack all 12 units right-side down, and turn so the light fabric just sewn is oriented above the previously sewn unit.

12. Place the next strip in the stack, dark fabric #1, right-side up in front of the needle. Pick up a sewn unit as shown above and put it on top of the dark fabric strip with right sides together, aligning the right side.

13. Sew to the end of the sewn unit, ensuring that the seam allowance is flat in the direction it was pressed. Add another sewn unit on top of the strip, right sides together, butting it to the end of the first sewn unit. Again, sew to the end of the sewn unit. Repeat until all 12 units are sewn to the dark fabric strips. If a strip will not accommodate a full unit, start another strip of the same fabric.

14. Trim the beginning and ending tail of the fabric strip just sewn.

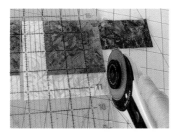

15. Cut the units apart where they butt up next to each other. Because the units were butted together for sewing, one cut will divide them evenly, leaving a trimmed straight edge.

16. Place each of the 12 units on the ironing board with the piece just sewn facing up. Press the seam, then flip the top fabric right-side up and press the unit open.

17. Stack all 12 units right-side down, and turn so the fabric just sewn is oriented above the previously sewn unit.

18. Continue adding strips until 2 strips of each fabric have been sewn, in the order they were stacked, to each unit. Each block should measure 10½" square.

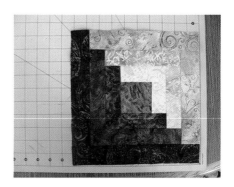

Diamond in the Square Block

The Diamond in the Square block is constructed using templates to cut the fabric. Templates are especially helpful for cutting odd, curved, or complicated shapes, or for fussy cutting a particular motif from the fabric pattern.

This block will use techniques already learned:

- Cutting fabrics accurately
- Sewing with a precise ¼" seam allowance
- Pressing seams
- Pressing seam allowances
- Making sure the seam allowance feeds through the machine in the direction it was pressed

The Diamond in the Square block will build upon them with new techniques:

- Using templates to cut fabric
- Pinning pieces before sewing
- Chain sewing

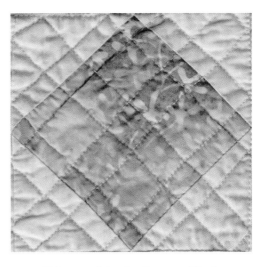

Diamond in the Square Block
Make 4

Cutting Instructions

Background Fabric #1 – Cut 16 triangles using the triangle template.

Light Fabric #2 – Cut 4 squares using the square template.

The diagram below shows the values of the Diamond in the Square block in black and white.

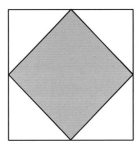

Assembling the Block

1. Set your printer to 100%, actual size. Print the templates on page 18. Cut out the templates. If a lot of pieces will be cut, make the template out of something sturdy like cardboard or plastic.

2. Trace around the templates on the wrong side of the fabric, using a sharp marking tool.

3. Cut out the fabric shapes using scissors.

4. With right sides together, place the long side of a triangle on one side of a square. Align the raw edges.

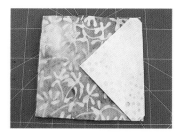

5. Pin the top, middle, and bottom with pins perpendicular to the edges.

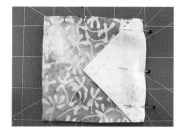

6. Sew, removing pins as they are reached.

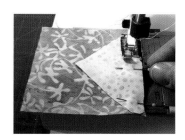

7. Do not remove the sewn unit from the machine. Feed the next paired unit into the sewing machine. This is called chain sewing, and it saves a lot of time when sewing many blocks. Once all 4 squares are sewn to a triangle, cut the threads, and remove the units from the machine.

8. Clip the threads between the units with scissors.

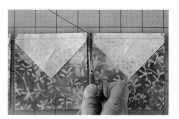

9. Place the units on the ironing board with the wrong side of the triangle facing up. Press the seam.

10. Flip the triangle piece right-side up and press the unit open.

11. Repeat until there are triangles sewn on all 4 sides of each square. Notice how the point of the square is ¼" from the edge of the unit. This will allow pieces to be sewn to this block without losing the point on the square.

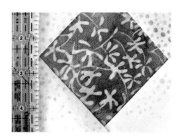

12. Give the blocks a final press. Each block should measure 4½" square.

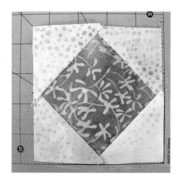

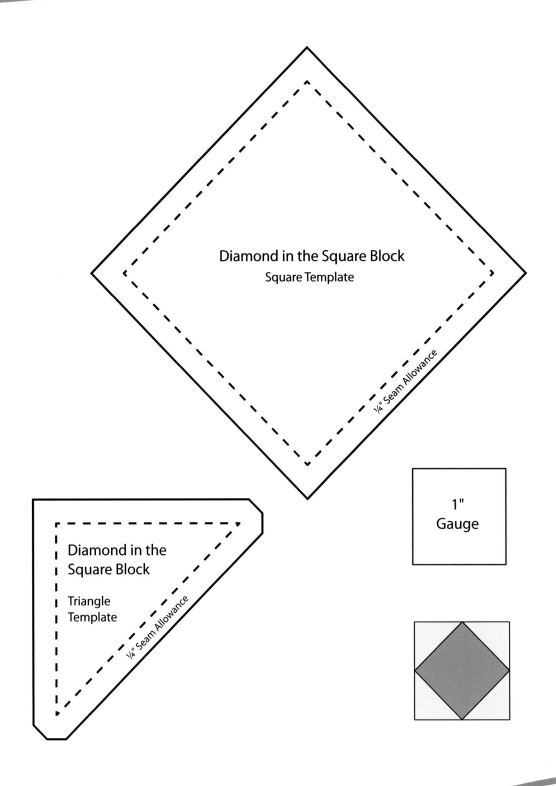

Diamond in the Square Block
Square Template

¼" Seam Allowance

Diamond in the
Square Block

Triangle
Template

¼" Seam Allowance

1"
Gauge

Quarter-Square Triangle Block

The Quarter-Square Triangle block will use traditional piecing techniques. These techniques are used in many quilts, whether in piecing or in the assembly of the blocks into the quilt top.

This block will use techniques already learned:

- Cutting fabrics accurately
- Sewing with a precise ¼" seam allowance
- Pressing seams
- Pressing seam allowances
- Making sure the seam allowance feeds through the machine in the direction it was pressed
- Pinning pieces before sewing
- Chain stitching

The Quarter-Square Triangle block will build upon them with these techniques:

- Sewing intersecting seams by nesting seam allowances
- Cutting tails

Quarter-Square Triangle Block
Make 16

Cutting Instructions

Background Fabric #1 - Cut (3) 11¼" strips.

Medium Fabric #2 - Cut (3) 11¼" strips.

The diagram below shows the values of the Quarter-Square Triangle block in black and white.

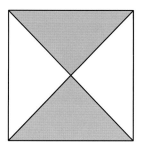

Assembling the Blocks

1. Cut the 11¼" strips into (8) 11¼" squares of each fabric.

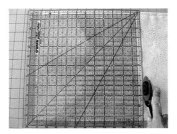

2. Cut the squares diagonally in each direction so 1 square yields 4 triangles. You need 32 triangles of each fabric.

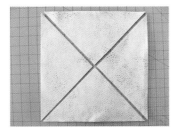

3. With right sides together, place a medium fabric triangle on top of a background fabric triangle. Align the edges.

4. Pin along one short side of the triangle at the top, middle, and bottom with the pins perpendicular to the edges. Sew, removing the pins as they are reached. Be careful to orient all the triangles the same way, sewing along the same short side. All double triangle units need to be identical and not mirror images of each other. Chain sew the triangles in pairs.

5. Cut the units apart.

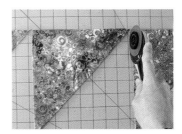

6. Place the units on the ironing board with the medium fabric facing up. Press the seam.

7. Flip the top fabric right-side up and press the unit open. This will press the seam allowance toward the medium fabric. If a pattern does not specify, press the seam allowance toward the darker fabric.

8. Once the 2 triangles are pieced together and pressed open, there will be a little tail on the end of the seams. This is because the corners were not blunted as they were when the triangles were cut from the template.

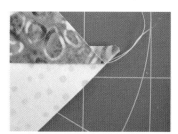

9. Cut the tail off so it does not get in the way when attaching this piece to another. Scissors or rotary cutters work fine.

10. Place 2 double triangle units right sides together so opposite fabrics stack on top of each other and outside edges are aligned. Sew along the long end of the triangle, over the seam of the already pieced triangles.

11. Because the seam allowances were pressed toward medium fabric #2, the seam allowances lie in opposite directions. This is called nesting the seam allowance. This is good for two reasons: 1) it helps lock the pieces in place so the seams meet, and 2) it distributes the bulk of the seam allowance to either side of the seam so there will not be a big hump on one side.

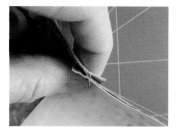

12. When the edges are aligned, pin the long side of the triangle at the top, on either side of the seam, and at the bottom.

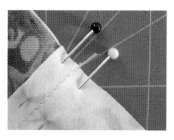

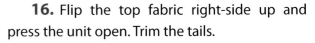

13. Sew, removing pins as they are reached. Feed the layered unit into the machine with the medium fabric on top and going first to ensure the top seam allowance goes under the needle in the direction it was pressed. The bottom seam allowance faces the opposite direction and will feed through the machine with no problem. Chain sew all the double triangle units into squares.

14. Cut the squares apart and make sure the seams are aligned.

15. Place the blocks on the ironing board. Press the seam.

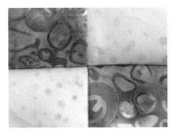

16. Flip the top fabric right-side up and press the unit open. Trim the tails.

17. Give the blocks a final press. Each block should measure 10½" square.

Flying Geese Block

I am going to present two different methods for piecing the Flying Geese unit. This unit is used as part of so many blocks that it warrants two methods. The method chosen may have to do with personal preference, the number of units needed, or the amount of fabric available for use. The Flying Geese unit is truly versatile. In this quilt, two Flying Geese units will be used to create the Flying Geese block. Read through all instructions before beginning the two methods as the cutting instructions are detailed and separate.

The Flying Geese blocks will use techniques already learned:

- Cutting fabric accurately
- Sewing with a precise ¼" seam allowance
- Pressing seams
- Pressing seam allowances
- Making sure the seam allowance feeds through the machine in the direction it was pressed
- Pinning pieces before sewing
- Chain sewing

You will build upon them with the following new techniques:

- Marking seam line on wrong side of fabric
- Marking seam allowance line on wrong side of fabric
- Trimming unit with a pre-marked cutting tool

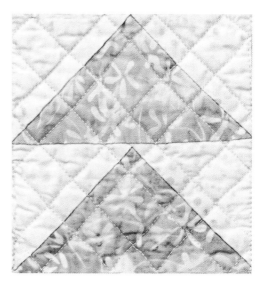

Flying Geese Block
Make 64

Method 1 Cutting Instructions

More fabric strips will be cut after the two methods are tried:

Background Fabric #1 – Cut (2) 2½" WOF strips. Cut the strips into (32) 2½" squares.

Light Fabric #2 – Cut (2) 2½" WOF strips. Cut the strips into (16) 2½" x 4½" rectangles.

The diagram below shows the values of the Flying Geese block in black and white.

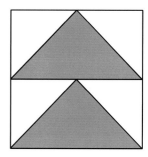

Method 1
Assembling Flying Geese Unit (Traditional Method)

Make 16

This method creates 1 Flying Geese unit at a time.

1. On the wrong side of each 1st background fabric square, mark a line diagonally through the square.

2. With right sides together, place a background fabric square on top of a light fabric rectangle so the diagonal goes from the center of the long side of the rectangle to the corner. Align 3 sides and, with the edges even, pin the square to the rectangle parallel to the diagonal line, but out of the way.

3. Using an open-toe foot, sew on the diagonal line. Chain sew a background fabric square onto each of the 16 light fabric rectangles. Remove pins.

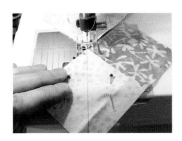

4. Cut the units apart.

5. Trim the seam allowance to ¼".

6. Place the units on the ironing board with the background fabric facing up. Press the seam.

7. Flip the top fabric right-side up and press the unit open.

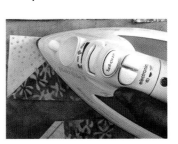

8. Repeat on the opposite side of the light fabric rectangle. With right sides together, place a background square on top of the other end of the light fabric rectangle, so the diagonal line goes from the center of the long side of the rectangle to the corner. Align 3 sides and the edges. Pin the square to the rectangle parallel to the diagonal line, but out of the way.

9. Sew on the diagonal line, making sure the seam allowance on the bottom side feeds through the machine in the direction it was pressed. Chain sew a background fabric square onto each of the units. Remove pins.

10. Cut the units apart. Trim seam allowance to ¼".

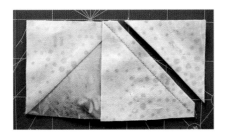

11. Place the units on the ironing board with the background fabric facing up. Press the seam.

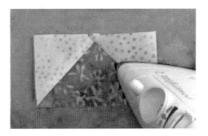

12. Flip the top fabric right-side up and press the unit open. This will press the seam allowance toward the background fabric.

13. Notice how the point of the triangle is ¼" from the edge of the unit. This will allow pieces to be sewn to this block without losing the point on the triangle.

14. Give a final press. Each unit should measure 4½" x 2½".

Method *2* *Cutting Instructions*

More fabric strips will be cut after both methods are tried:

Background Fabric #1 – Cut (1) 7" WOF strip. Cut the strip into (4) 7" squares.

Light Fabric #2 – Cut (1) 5½" WOF strip. Cut the strip into (4) 5½" squares.

Method *2*
Assembling Flying Geese Unit (Specialty Ruler Method)

Make 16

This method creates 4 Flying Geese units at a time.

1. On the wrong side of the light fabric 5½" squares, mark a line diagonally through the squares.

2. With right sides together, center each light fabric square on top of a background 7" square. Pin the squares together parallel to the diagonal line, but out of the way.

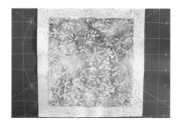

3. Sew ¼" from the diagonal line using the chain sewing method. Do not cut the units apart.

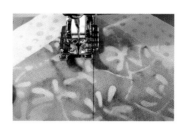

4. Repeat to sew ¼" from the other side of the diagonal line, using the chain-sewing method. Remove the pins after the square is sewn on both sides of the diagonal line.

5. Cut the units apart.

6. Press the units.

7. Cut each unit on the drawn diagonal line.

8. Place the units on the ironing board with the background fabric facing up. Flip the top fabric right-side up and press the unit open. This will press the seam allowance toward the background fabric.

9. On the wrong side of 8 of these pieced units, draw a diagonal line perpendicular to the seam.

10. With right sides together, place a marked unit on top of an unmarked unit so that opposite

fabrics stack on top of each other and the outside edges are aligned.

11. Pin the units together parallel to the diagonal line, but out of the way.

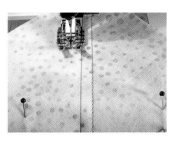

12. Sew ¼" away from the diagonal line in both directions using the chain-sewing method.

13. Remove the pins and cut the chained units apart. Press the seams.

14. Cut each unit on the diagonal line.

15. Clip the seam allowance in the middle of each unit.

16. Open the unit and place right-side down on the ironing board. Press the seam allowances so the light fabric triangle lies flat.

17. Align the red triangle on the specialty ruler with light fabric triangle in the unit. Trim on the 3 background fabric sides.

18. Reposition the speciality ruler and unit and make the final cut along the long side of the light fabric triangle. Repeat until all units are trimmed.

19. Give the units a final press. The units should measure 4½" x 2½" since they were cut after sewing.

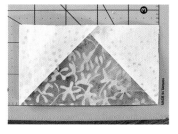

Creating Remaining Flying Geese Units

Make 96

Decide which method will be used to create the remaining units and follow the cutting instructions for that method.

METHOD 1 Cutting Instructions

Background Fabric #1 – Cut (12) 2½" WOF strips. Cut the strips into (192) 2½" squares.

Light Fabric #2 – Cut (12) 2½" WOF strips. Cut the strips into (96) 2½" x 4½" rectangles.

METHOD 2 Cutting Instructions

Background Fabric #1 – Cut (5) 7" WOF strips. Cut the strips into (24) 7" squares.

Light Fabric #2 – Cut (4) 5½" WOF strips. Cut the strips into (24) 5½" squares.

Assembling the Flying Geese Blocks

Make 64

1. Place 2 units as shown in the following photo.

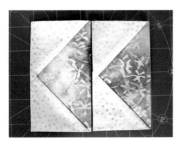

2. Bring the units right sides together, as if turning a page in a book. Pin the top, middle, and bottom perpendicular to the edges. Repeat steps 1 and 2 for all 64 blocks.

3. Using the chain-sewing method, sew the units in pairs using a ¼" seam allowance. Remove the pins as they are reached. Be careful to ensure that the seam allowances are lying flat, in the direction they were pressed, as they go through the machine.

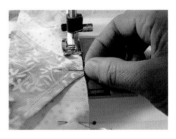

HINT: Be careful to sew across the existing seams at the point at which they cross. This will ensure the point of the triangle is not cut off.

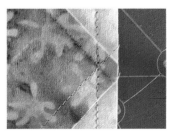

4. Cut the blocks apart.

5. Place the block on the ironing board with the triangle point toward you. Press the seam, then flip the top unit up and press the block open. Repeat for all 64 blocks.

Each block should measure 4½" square.

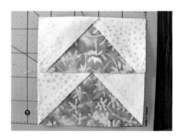

Pinwheel Blocks

I am going to present two different methods for piecing the half-square triangle unit which makes up the Pinwheel Block. This unit is used as part of so many blocks, it warrants two methods. The method chosen may have to do with personal preference, number of units needed, size of the quilt, or the amount of fabric to use. For this quilt, the large cornerstone Pinwheel blocks will be made using Method 1, a more traditional piecing method. The Multiple Pinwheel blocks will be made using Method 2, a printed pattern method. It requires less accuracy during construction, but yields a more accurate unit when completed. I have made entire quilts using just this unit. Four half-square triangle units are used to make the Large Pinwheel Block. Four Pinwheel units are used to make the Multiple Pinwheel block.

The Pinwheel block will use techniques already learned:
- Cutting fabric accurately
- Sewing with a precise ¼" seam allowance
- Pressing seams
- Pressing seam allowances
- Making sure the seam allowance feeds through the machine in the direction it was pressed
- Pinning pieces before sewing
- Chain sewing
- Cutting tails
- Marking seam allowance lines on wrong side of fabric.

You will build upon them with a new technique:
- Using patterns to sew half-square triangle units

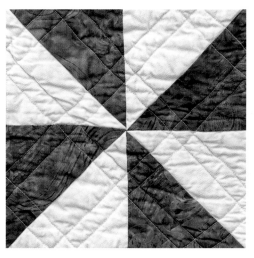

Large Pinwheel Block
Make 4

Multiple Pinwheel Block
Make 36

The diagram below shows the values of the single Pinwheel block in black and white.

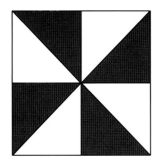

METHOD 1 *Cutting Instructions*

This method will be used to make the 16 Half-Square Triangle units needed to complete the 4 large Pinwheel cornerstone blocks.

Background Fabric #2 – Cut (1) 4⅞" WOF strip. Cut the strip into (8) 4⅞" squares.

Dark Fabric #2 – Cut (1) 4⅞" WOF strip. Cut the strip into (8) 4⅞" squares.

METHOD 1
Assembling Half-Square Triangle Units (Traditional Method)

Make 16

This method creates 2 half-square triangle units at a time.

1. On the wrong side of each background fabric square, mark a line diagonally through the squares.

2. With right sides together, place a background fabric square on top of a dark fabric square, aligning the edges.

3. Pin parallel to the diagonal line, but out of the way.

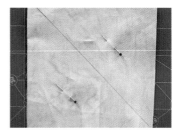

4. Use the chain-sewing method to sew ¼" away from the diagonal line as was done for Flying Geese. Do not cut the chains apart.

5. Repeat to sew ¼" away from the other side of the diagonal line using the chain-sewing method. Remove pins.

6. Cut the units apart.

7. Press the units.

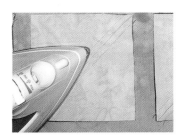

8. Cut each unit on the diagonal line.

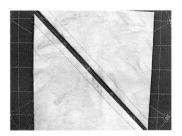

9. Place the units on the ironing board with the dark fabric facing up. Flip the top fabric right-side up and press the unit open. This will press the seam allowance toward the dark fabric.

10. Trim the tails from each unit.

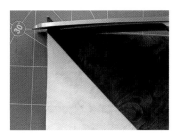

11. Give the units a final press. They should measure 4½" square. Set these units aside. The Large Pinwheel blocks will be made after completing method 2 units (see Assembling the Pinwheel Block starting on page 36).

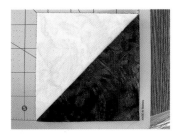

The diagram below shows the values of the Multiple Pinwheel block in black and white.

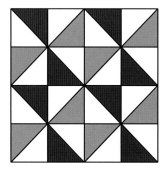

METHOD 2 *Cutting Instructions*

This method will be used to make the 608 half-square triangle units needed to make the 152 small Pinwheel blocks. Don't panic! With this method, I can make almost 100 half-square triangle units in about an hour.

Background Fabric #2 – Cut (7) 6½" WOF strips. Cut the strips into (27) 6½" x 9" rectangles.

Background Fabric #3 – Cut (6) 6½" WOF strips. Cut the strips into (24) 6½" x 9" rectangles.

Dark Fabric #1 – Cut (5) 6½" WOF strips. Cut the strips into (19) 6½" x 9" rectangles.

Dark Fabric #2 – Cut (4) 6½" WOF strips. Cut the strips into (16) 6½" x 9" rectangles.

Dark Fabric #3 – Cut (4) 6½" WOF strips. Cut the strips into (16) 6½" x 9" rectangles.

METHOD 2
Assembling Half-Square Triangle Units (Printed Pattern Method)
Make 608

1. Print 51 copies of the Half-Square Triangle units pattern on page 42. Regular copy paper will work just fine for this application. Trim each pattern down to about a 6½" x 9" rectangle. I find that the rotary cutter works great for this. Stack and cut up to 20 sheets of paper at a time. This pattern creates 12 half-square triangle units at a time.

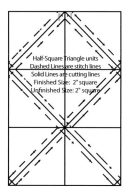

Half-Square Triangle units
Dashed Lines are stitch lines
Solid Lines are cutting lines
Finished Size: 2" square
Unfinished Size: 2" square

2. Place a background fabric rectangle on top of a dark fabric rectangle with right sides together. Place one pattern on top of this sandwich. Pin the layers together.

3. Sew on the dashed line. Begin at the point marked start, follow the direction of the arrows, and end at the point marked finish in one continuous line. Use an open-toe foot, a bigger needle (90/14), and a smaller stitch length (1 less than normal). At the corners, stop with the needle down, rotate the unit, and continue sewing on the dashed line. Since the pattern is rotated as it is sewn, this is not a good candidate for chain sewing. Once the point marked finish is reached, cut the threads and remove from the machine. Repeat this step until all 51 patterns are stitched.

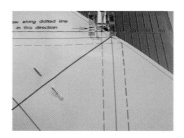

4. Remove pins. Press seams.

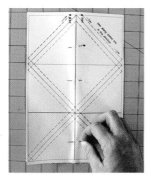

5. Cut the unit apart along the solid lines, starting with the perimeter, then the interior cross lines, and last the diagonal lines.

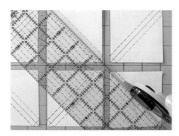

6. Place the units on the ironing board with the dark fabric facing up. Flip the top fabric right-side up and press the unit open. This will press the seam allowance toward the dark fabric.

7. Trim the tails.

8. Remove the paper pattern.

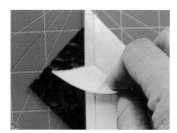

9. Give the 608 units a final press. Units should measure 2½" square. Set 4 units aside.

Assembling the Pinwheel Block

1. The half-square triangle units need to be sewn into pairs. Make the small Pinwheel units first. Make 2 piles (304 units each). Pile half the half-square triangle units with the dark fabric in the upper-right corner in the left pile and half with the dark fabric in the lower-right corner in the right pile.

2. Flip 1 unit from the right pile onto 1 unit in the left pile, as if you were turning a page in a book.

3. Pick up the 2 pieces which are now right sides together.

4. Nest the seam allowance of the diagonal seams and pin at the top and bottom of the right side.

5. Chain sew all the units together into pairs, removing the pins as they are reached. Be careful to ensure the seam allowances are lying flat in the direction they were pressed as they go through the machine.

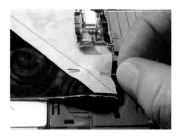

6. Cut the units apart.

7. Place the units on the ironing board with the unit having the seam in the dark fabric facing up. Press the seam.

8. Flip the top fabric right-side up and press the unit open. This will press the seam allowance to the dark fabric side.

9. Note how the point of the triangle is ¼" from the edge of the unit. This will allow pieces to be sewn to the block without losing the points on the triangles.

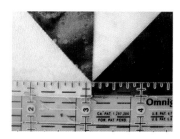

10. Make 2 piles (152 units each). Place the units with the dark fabric in the upper right and upper left corners in the left pile. Place the units with the dark fabric in the lower right and lower left corners in the right pile.

11. Flip 1 unit in the right pile onto 1 unit in the left pile, as if you were turning a page in a book. Pick up the 2 pieces which are now right sides together, nesting all the seam allowances.

12. Pin at the top, on either side of the center to ensure the seams meet in the middle, and at the bottom of the right side.

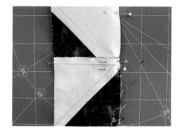

13. Check to see if all the seams meet in the middle.

14. Chain sew along the right side of the units, removing the pins as they are reached. Be careful to ensure the seam allowances are lying flat, in the direction they were pressed, as they go through the machine.

15. Cut the units apart.

16. Press the seams.

17. Open the unit and place it face down on the ironing board. Press the seam just sewn open. This will reduce the bulk in the center where all the seams come together.

18. Give the unit a final press. Small Pinwheel units should measure 4½" square. There should be (152) 4½" pinwheel units.

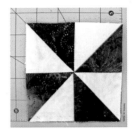

19. Repeat these steps, sewing the reserved 4½" half-square triangle units into (4) 8½" Pinwheel blocks. Set the large Pinwheel blocks aside.

Assembling the Mutiple Pinwheel Blocks
Make 36

1. Set 8 small pinwheel units aside. Place the remaining 144 small pinwheel units right-side up into 2 equal piles. The seam that was pressed open should be oriented horizontally.

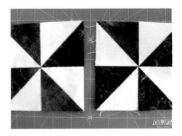

2. Flip 1 block from the right pile onto 1 block from the left pile, as if you were turning a page in a book.

3. Pick up the 2 pieces which are now right sides together. Nest all the seam allowances and pin at the top, on either side of the center seam, and the bottom of the right side. Repeat these steps for the remaining blocks.

4. Chain sew along the right side of the blocks, removing pins as they are reached. Be careful to ensure the seam allowances are lying flat, in the direction they were pressed, as they go through the machine. Cut the units apart. Check to make sure the seams meet in the middle.

5. Place the blocks on the ironing board. Press the seams.

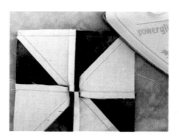

6. Flip the top fabric right-side up and press the unit open.

7. Make 2 equal piles of double pinwheel units with right sides facing up. The middle seam allowance on the left pile should be facing up.

8. The middle seam allowance on the right pile should be facing down.

9. Flip 1 unit in the right pile onto 1 unit in the left pile, as if you were turning the page of a book, nesting the seam allowances.

10. Pin at the top, on either side of each seam, and at the bottom of the right side. The challenge here is to get all the seams to meet in the middle.

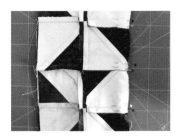

11. Chain sew along the right side of the blocks, removing the pins as they are reached. Be careful to ensure that the seam allowances are lying flat in the direction they were pressed, as they go through the machine. Cut the blocks apart.

12. Place the blocks on the ironing board. Press the seams.

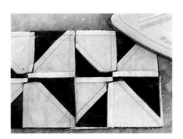

13. Open the block and place it right-side down on the ironing board. Press the seam just sewn open. This will reduce the bulk in the center where all the seams come together.

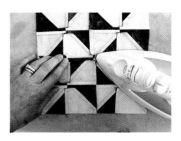

14. Give the blocks a final press. The Multiple Pinwheel blocks should measure 8½" square.

15. Using the 8 pinwheel units that were set aside in step 1, sew them into 4 pairs. This is a half Multiple Pinwheel block. Make 4.

Bonus – How to Draw a Grid for Creating Half-Square Triangles

1. Add ⅞" to the desired finished half-square triangle unit. For example, for a finished 1" size, draw a square 1⅞". Draw as many squares as desired, butting them together in pairs.

2. Draw a solid diagonal line through each square, consistent with the pattern shown. Draw a dashed parallel line ¼" on both sides of the diagonal lines. The dashed lines are the stitching lines. Place arrows as shown.

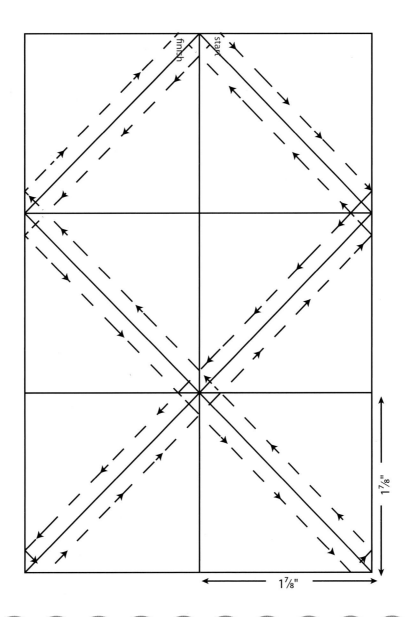

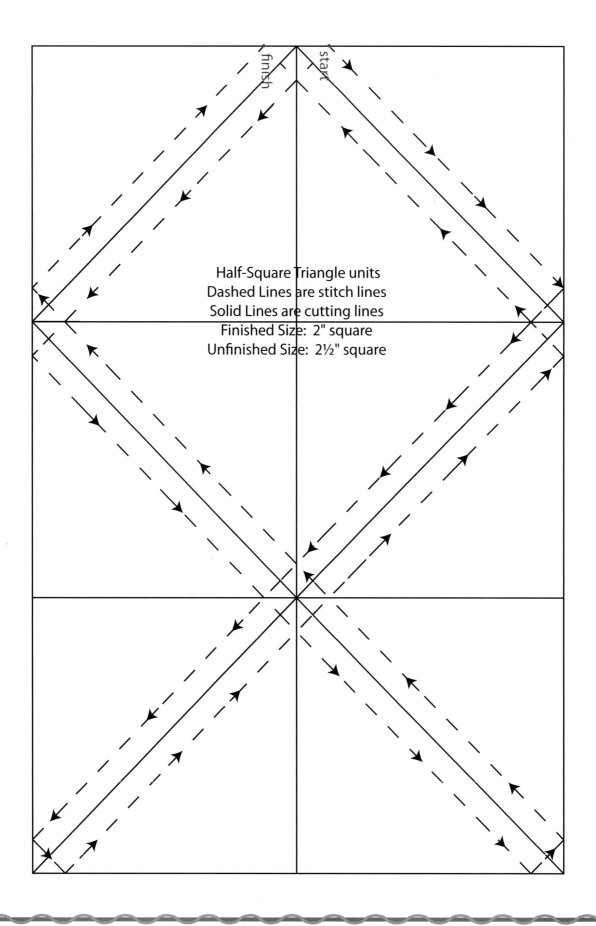

Half-Square Triangle units
Dashed Lines are stitch lines
Solid Lines are cutting lines
Finished Size: 2" square
Unfinished Size: 2½" square

Patchwork Square Block

Any of the traditional piecing methods learned so far could be used to make the Patchwork Square block. However, this block contains 100 pieces and that is a lot of seams to match up. Using the fusible interfacing method will speed up the piecing and create a more accurately finished block. This technique can be used on any block in which the rows and columns of sewing line up in both directions.

This Patchwork Square block will use some or all of these techniques already learned:
- Cutting fabric accurately
- Sewing with a precise ¼" seam allowance
- Pressing seams
- Pressing seam allowances
- Making sure the seam allowance feeds through the machine in the direction it was pressed
- Sewing intersecting seams by nesting seam allowances

You will build upon them with the following new technique:
- Using interfacing to place pieces of a block

Patchwork Square Block
Make 1

The diagram below shows the values of the Patchwork Square block in black and white.

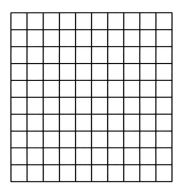

Cutting Instructions

Background Fabric #2 – Cut (4) 2½" WOF strips. Cut the strips into (50) 2½" squares.

Background Fabric #3 – Cut (4) 2½" WOF strips. Cut the strips into (50) 2½" squares.

Fusible Feather Weight Interfacing – Cut (2) 20" x 25" rectangles.

Assembling the Blocks

1. One 25" square of fusible interfacing is needed for this block. Most interfacing comes in a width smaller than 25" so two 20" x 25" rectangles will need to be joined to create the 25" width. Butt the two 25" sides together. Ensure the pieces are facing the same direction. Sew them together using a zigzag stitch. Trim interfacing to a 25" square.

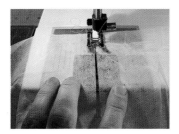

2. With a fine-line permanent marking pen, draw a 2½" spaced grid on the non-fusible side of the 25" square of interfacing. There should be (10) 2½" squares in both directions.

3. With the fusible side of the interfacing facing up, place the 2½" squares within the grid in the desired pattern, alternating background fabric #2 squares and background fabric #3 squares to form a checkerboard pattern.

4. Iron all the pieces into place.

5. Fold the unit right-sides together along one of the marked grid lines. Sew using a ¼" seam allowance.

6. Continue to fold and sew all the grid lines going in this same direction.

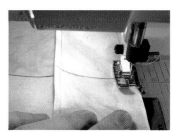

7. Press the seams just sewn.

8. Snip the seam allowance of the seams just sewn at each marked line that is perpendicular to the seams. Be careful not to snip the stitching.

9. Fold the unit along the first seam just snipped, i.e., going in the opposite direction of the first set of seams already stitched. Sew, nesting the seams as they are sewn. For the first seam in this direction, sew with the top seam allowance facing up and the bottom seam allowance facing down.

10. For the next seam, sew with the top seam allowance facing down and the bottom seam allowance facing up. Continue sewing the seams, alternating the seam allowances until all seams are sewn.

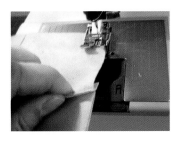

11. Press each seam.

12. Press all the seams in one direction from the back side.

13. Give the block a final press. The block should measure 20½" square.

Note how perfectly the seams line up.

Twelve Triangles Block

The Twelve Triangles block will be constructed using paper piecing techniques. This technique results in absolutely perfect points and sized blocks.

This block will use some or all of these techniques already learned:

- Cutting fabric accurately
- Pressing seams
- Pressing seam allowances
- Making sure the seam allowance feeds through the machine in the direction it was pressed
- Chain sewing

This block will build upon them with the following new technique:

- Paper piecing

The diagram below shows the values of the Twelve Triangles block in black and white.

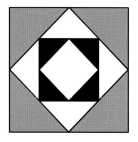

Twelve Triangles Block
Make 4

Cutting Instructions

Background Fabric #1 – Cut (1) 4½" WOF strip. Cut (4) 4½" squares from the strip to be for piece 1.

Background Fabric #2 – Cut (1) 4¾" WOF strip. Cut the strip into (8) 4¾" squares. Cut the squares in half diagonally to create 16 triangles to be used for pieces 6, 7, 8, and 9.

Medium Fabric #2 – Cut (2) 6¼" WOF strips. Cut the strips into (8) 6¼" squares. Cut the squares in half diagonally to create 16 triangles to be used for pieces 10, 11, 12, and 13.

Dark Fabric #1 – Cut (1) 3¾" WOF strip. Cut the strip into (8) 3¾" squares. Cut the squares in half diagonally to create 16 triangles to be used for pieces 2, 3, 4, and 5.

Assembling the Blocks

1. Place 1 of the printed block patterns (page 50) face down. Position 1 background fabric square #1 right-side up over area 1. Use a dab of fabric glue to hold it in place.

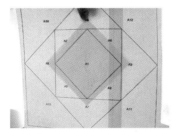

2. Turn the pattern over so the printed side is up. Hold it to the light to check that the fabric is centered over area 1.

3. Pin in place on the printed side of the pattern with pin parallel to the first seam (line between location 1 and 2).

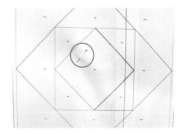

4. Place the pattern on a cutting mat with printed-side up. Align a cardboard edge along the first sewing line (between location 1 and 2).

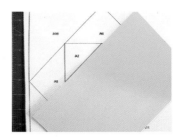

5. Fold the pattern back over the cardboard.

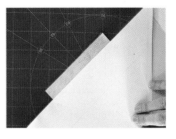

6. Measure ¼" from the fold (sewing line) and cut the fabric. I like to use a ruler designed to add a ¼" (Add-A-Quarter™ ruler), but any measuring ruler will work. This cut provides a ¼" seam allowance and gives an edge to align the next piece of fabric.

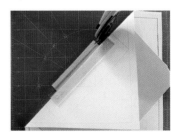

7. Turn the pattern over so the printed side is down and the fabric is facing up. Place a dark fabric triangle piece right-side up over area 2, then flip it right sides together, aligning the raw edges as shown. This is along the stitch line between areas 1 and 2. Pin in place.

8. Turn the pattern printed-side up. Sew along the line between areas 1 and 2, starting and stopping ¼" before and after the line. Use an open-toe foot, a larger needle (90/12), and a smaller stitch length (1 whole number less) to make pattern removal easier.

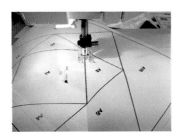

9. Remove pins and press the seam. Do not use steam to press as this can distort the paper pattern.

10. Flip the top fabric right-side up and press the unit open.

11. Repeat these steps, working around the pattern in numerical order for areas 3 through 13. See cutting instructions for fabric placement.

12. Once all pieces are sewn and pressed, pin to hold the outside fabric triangles in place and turn the block, printed pattern face up. Trim all layers on the dashed line. This will allow for a ¼" seam allowance around the block.

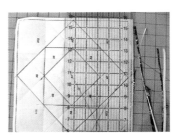

13. Remove the paper. Optional: Paper can be left in place until the block is sewn into the quilt, then removed.

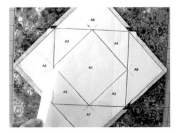

14. Give it a final press. The block should measure 10½" square.

Additional Info Section - Calculating Piece Size for Paper Piecing

1. For all shapes within a pattern, except for triangles, measure the widest part of both the length and width of each area. Add ¾" to each of these measurements. This is the size to cut the piece. This shape will provide the needed ¼" seam allowance plus an additional ¼" for safety. For the following example, cut the piece 5" x 9¼".

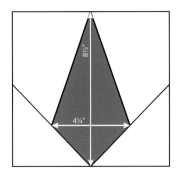

2. For triangular-shaped areas, cut a triangular piece of fabric instead of a rectangle. Measure the short sides of the triangle and add 1¼". This is the size to cut the square, then cut the square in half diagonally. For the following example, cut the square 5½".

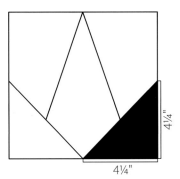

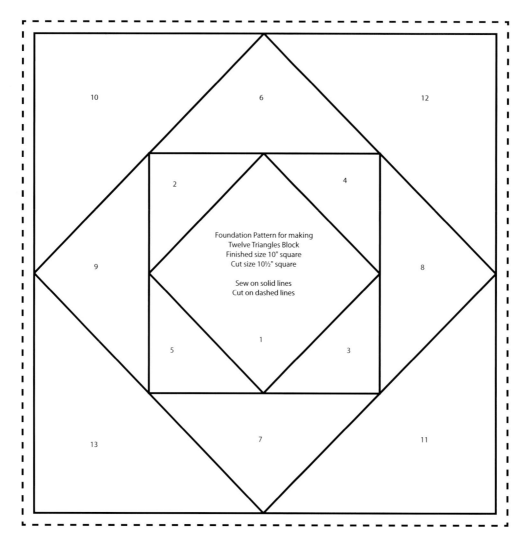

Foundation Pattern for making
Twelve Triangles Block
Finished size 10" square
Cut size 10½" square

Sew on solid lines
Cut on dashed lines

Enlarge pattern 200%
Make 4 copies

Raw-Edge Appliqué

The raw-edge appliqué will be stitched on the Patchwork Square block. A traditional wreath pattern will be used. The technique for this block will be a raw-edge machine stitch that is quick and easy.

Raw-edge appliqué will use techniques already learned:

- Making templates to cut fabric
- Using interfacing to layout pieces of a block

You will build upon them with a new technique:

- Machine stitching the raw edge of fabric to sew it in place

Center Block
Make 1

Cutting Instructions

Gather fabric from your stash of various colors and values that coordinate with the fabrics used in your quilt for the pieces of the appliqué.

Fusible Feather Weight Interfacing –
Cut (1) 20" square.

The photograph below shows the values of the appliqué in black and white.

Appliqué Instructions

1. Copy the template (page 55) at 100%, actual size, on to the paper side of the iron-on adhesive paper. I like to use Therm O Web HeatnBond® Lite paper. The templates can also be traced onto the paper side of the adhesive. Make 4 copies of each template.

2. Place the square of fusible interfacing on top of the wreath layout pattern with the fusible side facing down. Trace the pattern (page 54) onto the fusible interfacing.

3. Fuse the interfacing pattern to the wrong side of the Patchwork Square block. This will be used as a guide for placing the fabric pieces. The advantage of tracing the pattern onto interfacing and adhering to the wrong side of the block is that the fabric pieces can be pressed into place without a paper pattern shifting or shrinking with the heat or steam of an iron.

4. Roughly cut out the adhesive paper pattern pieces and iron them onto the wrong side of the desired fabric.

5. Cut the fabric pieces out precisely on the line.

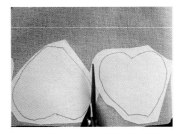

6. Remove the paper from the piece, exposing the adhesive.

7. Place the Patchwork Square block on a light table right-side up and the interfacing pattern face down. Place each fabric piece adhesive-side down, onto the block in the appropriate place. Overlap fabric as shown in the wreath layout pattern, then press Into place.

8. Once all pieces are pressed in place, remove the interfacing pattern from the wrong side.

9. Give the block a good final pressing on the ironing board.

10. To permanently hold the fabric pieces in place and to prevent them from fraying, machine stitch around the edge of each piece to appliqué them in place. Use a smaller needle (size 70/11 or 60/10) so it doesn't splinter the fabric.

"My favorite stitches for appliqué are the straight stitch, the blanket stitch (used for the stems and leaves), and the zigzag or satin stitch (used for the flowers)."

The appliqué stitching should secure just the edge of the piece of fabric. Position the presser foot so the right swing of the stitch will be next to the edge of the fabric, and the left swing of the stitch will "bite" into the fabric.

Tips for Machine Appliqué

When stitching around the edge of the piece, using the zigzag stitch remember if you are stitching an outside corner or edge or turning the fabric in a counterclockwise direction, make sure to stop with the needle in the down position on the right swing of the stitch before pivoting your fabric. The tighter the radius on a curve, the more times you will have to pivot the fabric.

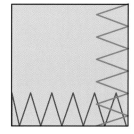

Conversely, if you are stitching an inside corner or edge or turning the fabric in a clockwise direction, make sure to stop with the needle in the down position on the left swing of the stitch before pivoting your fabric. Always try to keep the "bite" perpendicular to the fabric edge.

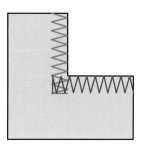

When stitching around the edge of the piece with the blanket stitch, remember to pivot the fabric after the stitch "bites" into the fabric and the needle is back out along the edge of the fabric again. If the fabric is pivoted in the middle of a "bite" it will have a gap in the swing stitches.

The easiest place to start the stitching is along a continuous line. It is more difficult to start at an inner or outer point. The length and width of a stitch used for appliqué will depend on the size of the piece of fabric being sewn. On larger pieces use a longer and wider stitch; however, on smaller pieces use a shorter and narrower stitch.

Layout pattern. Enlarge template 400%

1"
Gauge

BUILDING BLOCKS Quilt
Print 4 copies
Raw Edge Applique Templates
Designed by Diane Califano

Template pieces shown at 100%

Assembling the Quilt Top

Blocks will be sewn together and block strips will be created while the quilt top is assembled. Please read all instructions before beginning.

Using the techniques learned throughout the completion of the blocks, strips will be sewn. Remember:

- Pin at the beginning, end, and at all critical seam intersections, nesting seam allowances whenever possible.
- Sew with a precise ¼" seam allowance, removing pins when they are reached and the seam allowance feeds through the machine in the direction it was pressed on both the top and bottom pieces.
- Chain sew blocks together to speed the sewing process.
- Press each seam.
- Press the seam allowance in the desired direction.

Log Cabin Blocks

1. Sew 2 Log Cabin blocks into a 2-block strip as shown below. Press the seams, then press the seam allowances to one side. The unit should measure 10½" x 20½".

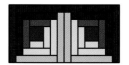

Make 4.

2. Sew a Log Cabin block to each end of 2 of the 2-block strips as shown. Press the seams, then press the seam allowances to one side. The strip should measure 10½" x 40½".

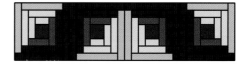

Make 2.

Quarter-Square Triangle Blocks

1. Sew all 16 of the Quarter-Square Triangle blocks into eight 2-block strips. Press the seam, then press the seam allowance to one side. The unit should measure 10½" x 20½".

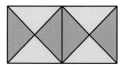

Make 8.

2. Sew the 2-block strips into (4) 4-block strips. Press the seams, then press the seam allowance to one side. Each strip should measure 10½" x 40½".

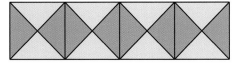

Make 4.

3. Sew one Twelve Triangles block to each end of 2 of the 4-block strips. Press the seams, then press the seam allowances toward each Twelve Triangles block. Each of these strips should measure 10½" x 60½".

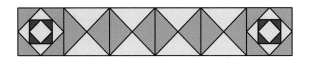

Make 2.

Flying Geese Blocks

1. Sew the 64 Flying Geese blocks into (32) 2-block strips. Remember that each Flying Geese block has 2 Flying Geese units. Press the seam, then press the seam allowance toward the point of the triangles. Each unit should measure 4½" x 8½".

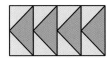

Make 32.

2. Sew the (32) 2-block strips into (16) 4-block strips. Press the seam, then press the seam allowance toward the point. Each strip should measure 4½" x 16½".

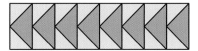

Make 16.

3. Sew the (16) 4-block strips into (8) 8-block strips. Press the seam, then press the seam allowance toward the point. Each strip should measure 4½" x 32½".

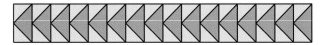

Make 8.

4. Sew the (8) 8-block strips into (4) 16-block strips, with 1 set of 8-blocks pointing left and 1 set pointing right. Press the seams, then press all but the center seam allowance toward the point of the triangles. Press the center seam allowance open. Each strip should measure 4½" x 64½". Make note of this measurement.

Make 4.

5. Sew 1 Diamond in the Square block to each end of 2 of the 16-block strips. Press the seams, then press the seam allowances toward the Diamond in a Square block. Each piece should measure 4½" x 72½".

Make 2.

6. For the 2 Flying Geese strips that did not have a Diamond in the Square block sewn to them, repress the very last seam allowance on both ends so they go toward the center of the strip. This will help nest seam allowances when the strips are attached to the quilt top.

Pinwheel Blocks

1. Sew 32 of the Multiple Pinwheel blocks into (16) 2-block strips. Make sure that the seam allowances that were pressed open are oriented parallel to the seam that will be sewn to join the blocks. This way the seams that were perpendicular can be nested. Each strip should measure 8½" x 16½".

Make 16.

2. Sew each of the remaining 4 Multiple Pinwheel blocks to a half Multiple Pinwheel block to create a block-and-a-half strip. Make sure the seam allowances that were pressed open are oriented parallel to the seam that will be sewn to join the blocks. Each strip should measure 8½" x 12½".

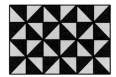

Make 4.

3. Sew the (16) 2-block strips into (8) 4-block strips. Each strip should measure 8½" x 32½".

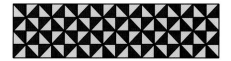

Make 8.

4. Sew the (8) 4-block strips into (4) 8-block strips. Press the seams, then press the seam allowances open to reduce the bulk in the seam. Each strip should measure 8½" x 64½".

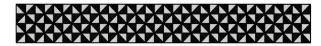

Make 4.

5. Sew 1 block-and-a-half strip to each of the 8-block strips. Press the seam, then press the seam allowances open to reduce bulk in the seam. Each strip should measure 8½" x 76½". Make note of this measurement.

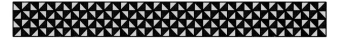

Make 4.

6. Sew 1 large Pinwheel block to each end of 2 of the 9½-block strips, orienting the block as necessary to nest the seam allowances. Press the seams, then press the seam allowances toward the larger Pinwheel block. Each strip should measure 8½" x 92½".

Make 2.

7. For the 2 multiple Pinwheel block strips that did not get a larger Pinwheel block sewn to them, repress the very last seam allowance on both ends so they go toward the center of the strip. This will help nest seam allowances when the strips are attached to the quilt top.

Attaching Block Strips Together

As the block strips are sewn together to form the quilt top, remember:

- Pin at the beginning, end, and at all critical seam intersections, nesting seam allowances whenever possible.
- Sew with a precise ¼" seam allowance, removing pins when they are reached and the seam allowance feeds through the machine in the direction it was pressed on both the top and bottom pieces
- Press each seam.
- Press the seam allowance in the desired location.
- If one strip is slightly longer than the strip it is being attached to, put the longer strip on the bottom. As it is fed through the machine, the feed dogs will pull on the bottom layer slightly quicker, easing in the fullness.

1. Starting with the Patchwork Square block (shown without the appliqué for clarity), attach a Log Cabin 2-block strip to each side, nesting seam allowances as possible. Press the seams, then press the seam allowances toward the Log Cabin blocks. This section should measure 20½" x 40½".

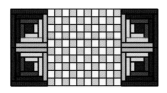

2. Attach a Log Cabin 4-block strip to the top and bottom. Press the seams, then press the seam allowances toward the Log Cabin 4-block strips. This section should measure 40½" square.

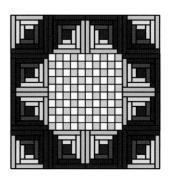

3. Attach a Quarter-Square Triangle 4-block strip to each side. Orient the strip as necessary to nest the seam allowances. Press the seams, then press the seam allowances toward the Log Cabin blocks. This section should measure 40½" x 60½".

4. Attach the strip of the 4 Quarter-Square Triangle blocks with the Twelve Triangles block on each end to the top and bottom. Orient the strip as necessary to nest the seam allowances. Press the seams, then press the seam allowances toward the Log Cabin blocks. This section should measure 60½" square. Make note of this measurement.

Straight Borders and Remaining Pieced Borders

NOTE: Adjustments may be necessary if a quilt's measurements are different from the instruction measurements. Measure the quilt top vertically and horizontally across the center. Subtract this measurement from the length of the side border strips of the pieced border that will be placed on the outside of the plain, straight border. Divide by 2, then add ½" for seam allowance. This is the width to cut the strips for the straight border. Substitute this width for the width given. Adjust the length of the strips to fit as necessary.

1. For the first border, cut (7) 2½" WOF strips from medium fabric #1 (adjust width if necessary). Sew the strips together into one continuous piece, using a 45° seam. Place 2 strips right sides together at 90° to each other. Pin them together, then draw a 45° line where the strips intersect. Sew on the line. Press. Trim the seam allowance to ¼" then press the seam open.

2. Cut (2) 60½" x 2½" strips, and (2) 64½" x 2½" strips (adjust strip length to match pieced border as necessary). Sew the (2) 60½" long strips to the sides of the quilt. Press the seams, then press the seam allowances toward the border strips. The quilt top should measure 60½" x 64½".

3. Sew the (2) 64½" long strips to the top and bottom of the quilt. Press the seams, then press the seam allowances toward the border strips. The quilt top should measure 64½" square.

4. Sew 1 Flying Geese 16-block strip to each side of the quilt top. Press the seams, then press the seam allowances toward the straight borders. The quilt top should measure 64½" x 72½".

the seam allowances toward the straight border. The quilt top should measure 72½" x 76½".

5. Sew 1 Flying Geese 16-block strip with the Diamond in the Square block on either end to the top and bottom of the quilt top. Press the seams, then press the seam allowances toward the straight borders. The quilt top should measure 72½" square.

7. Sew the 76½" strips to the top and bottom of the quilt top. Press the seams, then press the seam allowances toward the straight border. The quilt top should measure 76½" square.

6. Cut (8) 2½" WOF strips from the light fabric #3 for the second straight border (measure and adjust width of strips if necessary). This border will be constructed in the same manner as the first straight border. After sewing the strips together, cut (2) 72½" x 2½" strips and (2) 76½" x 2½" strips (adjust length of strips to match pieced border if necessary). Sew the 72½" strips to the sides of the quilt top. Press the seams, then press

8. Attach 1 Multiple Pinwheel 9½-block strip to each side of the quilt top. Press the seams, then press the seam allowances toward the straight borders. The quilt top should measure 76½" x 92½".

9. Attach 1 Multiple Pinwheel 9½-block strip with the large Pinwheel blocks on each end to the top and bottom of the quilt top. Press the seams, then press the seam allowances toward the straight borders. The quilt top should measure 92½" square.

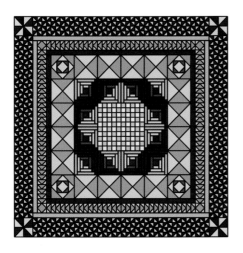

Straight Border with Mitered Corners

1. The third straight border is different from the other straight borders because it has mitered corners. For this technique the border fabric must be precut to the appropriate length before it is attached to the quilt top. Cut (10) 4"

WOF strips from the medium fabric #3. Sew 2 sets of 5 border strips, each in the same manner as the other straight borders. Cut each strip into 2 equal parts. Measure the quilt vertically and horizontally.

2. Cut each strip at a 45⁰ angle on one end as shown in the first photo below. Measure from the short side of the border 92½" (adjust length to match pieced border if necessary) and cut another 45⁰ angle as shown. This should be a mirror image of the first angle cut. Repeat this step on each of the other border strips.

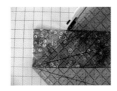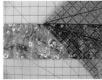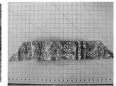

3. On the wrong side of the fabric, mark the short side of each strip ¼" from the beginning and ending of the strip. With right sides together, pin a border strip on each side of the quilt top. Align the short side with the edge of the quilt. See the photos below.

4. Once all the border pieces are sewn on, sew the mitered corner. Align the angle cut of adjacent border pieces, right sides together. Pin in place. Starting at the ¼" mark on the short side of the border strip, sew along the 45⁰ angle out to the long side of the border piece as shown below. Press the mitered seam open.

5. Press the seam along the quilt. Press the seam allowance toward the last border. The quilt top is done and should measure 100" square.

Building Blocks Quilt

Designing and Marking the Quilting

Now that the quilt top is done, it needs to be marked for quilting. Please read the entire set of instructions before doing any marking on the quilt top.

I know what you are thinking: "I spent so much time on this quilt top, I do not want to ruin it with my quilting." I know this because I have been there. Every new quilter has been there. Let me encourage you to quilt the tops as you make them. That way your quilting skills will progress right along with your piecing skills. It would be a shame to be a master piecer and then have to rely on someone else to do the quilting. I find quilting every bit the creative outlet and craft challenge as the making of the quilt top. With a few tips and some experience, I hope you will find the same to be true for you.

Things to keep in mind when designing the quilting:

- Quilting will be lost in busy fabric. For this reason, do not put a complicated quilting design on a busy fabric. All effort will be lost because the quilting design will be overpowered by the busy pattern and won't show up.

- Do not select a quilting design that puts stitching through an already bulky area. For example, on this quilt I chose a quilting pattern that did not go through the center of the pinwheels, as this area is already bulky with seam allowances. Sewing through a bulky area may cause the machine to skip stitches.

- If possible, select a quilting pattern for use in the center of the quilt that can be freemotion quilted. This way the entire quilt won't have to be turned through the sewing machine.

It is very helpful to audition the patterns for quilting before they are marked on the quilt top. That way you can verify you like them and check that the scale will correctly fill the space. You can do this with tracing paper, but I have found that Glad® Press'n Seal works great. It is clear and just a little sticky. You can place it over your pattern, trace, then peel it up and put it on the quilt as shown below. It will remain until you peel it up and move it. If the size of the pattern is not right, most of today's printers will allow printing another copy at a different scale.

When I am using the geometric patterns created by the piecing to inspire my quilting design, I place the "Press-n-Seal" on the quilt top and mark the design. This way I can pick up the pattern I have created and reposition it on the quilt to see what other effects I can get from the pattern. I can see how it can apply in other areas of the quilt. Repeating quilting patterns and motifs throughout the quilt is a good way to unify the quilting design.

- Center the pattern in each of the Log Cabin blocks as shown in the following photos.
- Center the pattern in each of the medium colored diamonds formed by the Quarter-Square Triangle blocks. Add half-of-a-pattern to the Quarter-Square Triangle blocks at the ends.
- Center the pattern in each of the corner Twelve Triangles blocks.

  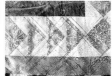   

For this quilt, I decided to quilt as follows:

Center Appliqué and Patchwork Squares Block

Quilt an outline ⅛" away from the inside and outside edges of the appliqué wreath. Also mark approximately ¼" away from the seam lines of the background Patchwork Square.

Log Cabin, Quarter-Square Triangles, and Twelve Triangles Blocks

Quilt a block-sized continuous line motif. See the 10" quilting template (page 69). Position the template, as described, onto the quilt top:

Borders

Quilt straight lines with varying widths of space in between. I do not mark these lines, but use the edge of my walking foot to keep the lines straight.

Flying Geese, Diamond in the Square, and Pinwheel Blocks

Quilt approximately ¼" away from the seam-lines in a cross-hatch geometric design that relates to the lines of the blocks. This is similar to the sewing pattern we used to sew the small half-square triangles for the Multiple Pinwheel blocks.

Marking the Quilt Top

The quilt top needs to be marked with the chosen patterns. There are several ways to mark a quilt for quilting. I am going to go over a few of my favorites. All of these techniques have their advantages, but they are a matter of personal preference. Try a few of these techniques when marking the quilt to see which ones you like the best.

I like to mark as much of my quilt top as I can before it is sandwiched, because it is easier to mark the fabric without the bulk of the backing and batting underneath. When I mark my quilt before sandwiching, I do not use a disappearing or vanishing ink pen. Those pen marks can disappear before the quilting is done. I also will not use chalk or a pounce as they tend to rub off with all the manipulating of the quilt through the sandwiching process.

I have had the best luck with the thermo-sensitive Pilot® Frixion® pens, Washable Graphite and Soapstone Markers by Morgan, and Fabric Pencils by Sewline®. Neither of the latter will set if ironed and both wash out with soap and water. The Frixion pen markings are easily removed with a hot iron. Whatever product you are using, always test to make sure it can be removed! There are new products constantly coming on the market, so don't be afraid to try different things to see how they work.

Drawing Directly onto the Quilt Top

I like to mark the geometric patterns on the quilt top before it is sandwiched. I do this by simply using a ruler and marking my lines directly onto the quilt top. I like this technique because there are no patterns to remove after quilting. I used this technique for the center appliqué, Patchwork Square, Flying Geese, Diamond in the Square, and Pinwheel blocks.

 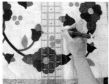 

Using a Light Table

This technique must be done before the quilt is sandwiched with the backing and batting. Once you have selected your quilting design and have scaled it to the desired size, put it on a light table and trace over the design with a dark marker so it will show through the fabric. Then, overlay the quilt top and trace the pattern onto the quilt top. I especially like this method because there are no patterns to remove after the quilting. I used this technique for the Log Cabin, Quarter Square Triangle, and Twelve Triangles blocks.

Other Methods

I would also like to demonstrate other methods of marking a quilt top in case a light table is not feasible nor desirable. I recommend using the following methods after the quilt is sandwiched together as the manipulating of the quilt through the sandwiching process may compromise the integrity of the markings.

Needle Punch Templates

This technique is especially helpful if there is a repeating motif in the quilt. Once the quilting motif is selected and scaled to the appropriate size, put it on top of a stack of 20 or so pieces of waxed or tracing paper. Staple the stack together with the pattern on top. On the sewing machine, use a large unthreaded needle (size 90/14 or larger) and sew along the outline of the pattern. Tear one pattern piece off at a time and pin it to the quilt top. Sew over the paper, using the holes in the pattern as a guide for the quilting. Once the quilting is done, remove the paper pattern. The biggest drawback to this method is that the removal of the paper pattern can be tedious.

Stencils and Pounce

This technique is especially helpful if you are marking on all dark fabric with white powder, or all light fabric with the blue powder. Position a stencil or needle punch template on the quilt top and wipe over it with the Pounce™ pad. If you are using the needle-punch template it is helpful to have the prickly side of the template facing upward so that it can "tickle" the pad and encourage the powder to drop onto the fabric. The biggest drawback to this technique is that the powder can rub off before the quilting can be done. That is why I like to use the Pounce pad in one area at a time.

Press'n Seal

This technique is especially helpful for doing borders. Once the border pattern is the appropriate scale to fit the width of the border, it does not necessarily fit the length of the border. Trace the scaled pattern onto the Press'n Seal, place it on the quilt, and adjust the spacing of the design to fit the length. Do this by simply cutting the Press'n Seal pattern and adjusting the location of the pattern either closer together, or further apart. This avoids having to completely redraw the pattern to adjust the spacing. The biggest drawback to this technique is that the glue from the Press'n Seal can collect on the needle and cause the machine to skip stitches. It also needs to be removed once the quilting is finished.

Quilting pattern. Enlarge 200%

1"
Square

Quilting and Binding

Once the quilting is designed and marked, the quilt can be "sandwiched" by layering the backing, batting, and top. Instructions for this are for machine quilting on a domestic machine. Please read the entire set of instructions before beginning.

Backing

When I select the backing fabric for my quilts, I like to select a fabric that will match the color of thread I will be using for the quilting. This way, the top and bobbin threads will match and disguises minor thread tension problems that can appear on the quilt.

It is also important to consider the pattern of the backing fabric:
- A busy pattern fabric will camouflage the quilting.
- A plain fabric will showcase the quilting.

I spend a lot of time quilting my quilts. I like to be able to see the finished quilting. For this reason I choose a plain fabric for my backing. If you are not yet confident in your quilting ability, you may want to consider a busier fabric for your backing. A busier fabric will hide the imperfections of a new quilter.

Another thing to consider in selecting the backing fabric is the fabric width. It is a good idea for the backing to be at least 6" wider and longer than the quilt top. If you select standard quilting fabric, you will need to piece 3 sections together to get a piece big enough for the backing of the quilt. This can easily be done by cutting 3 pieces, each at least 106" long, then sewing them together along the 106" long sides and cutting the 2 outside pieces down to make a 106" square piece of fabric. There is backing fabric available that is extra wide, eliminating the need for piecing the backing.

Once the fabric is selected you will want to treat it the same way you treated your quilt top fabrics. I prewash, press, and starch my quilt top fabrics. I do the same with my backing fabric.

Once it is prepared, I place it on a flat surface, which is usually the floor, and tape it on all 4 sides. As I tape it, I pull it taut, but do not stretch it. This will eliminate minor wrinkles and prevent puckering as you quilt. See the following photos.

Basting

The quilt layers need to be basted so they stay together during the quilting process. The most popular ways to baste a quilt include:

- Use thread basting, by hand, with a very large stitch length, after the layers are together.
- Use pin basting, with straight or safety pins, after the layers are together.
- Use spray basting, with an aerosol adhesive, as you layer.

My preferred method is basting with a spray adhesive. It seems to be quicker, easier, and it does not get in the way when I am quilting, nor does it require removal after quilting. I have used this method on quilts ranging in size from the very small to the very large and have always had good luck. However, I think the type of adhesive you use can make a difference. I have had very good luck with Sullivans® "Original" Quilt Basting Spray in the pink can.

As you layer the quilt, make sure to remove any stray pieces of thread or lint that may show through the quilt once it is complete. I find a tape roller lint remover works great for this. After I remove all the lint on the backing (that I have taped to the floor), I spray the backing with the basting spray as shown below.

Batting

There are several types of batting varying from cotton to wool to synthetic. They vary in warmth, loft, and density as well as many other properties. In this space I cannot detail all the types of batting. You may have to research several kinds to find your preference. For this quilt, I used an all-cotton Warm & Natural® brand batting. I like Warm & Natural because it is easy to work with on the machine, requires no prewashing, and seems to work well for both large and small quilts.

Once the spray adhesive on the backing has dried for about 10 minutes, I layer the batting on top of the backing. I like to start at one end, anchoring the leading edge by taping it to the floor. I unroll the batting a little at a time and smooth the fullness to the outside edges as shown.

Layering

With the batting lying smoothly on top of the backing, I remove any stray pieces of lint and then spray the batting with the basting spray.

Again, once the spray adhesive on the batting has dried for about 10 minutes, I layer the quilt top on top of the batting. I like to start at one end, anchoring the leading edge by taping it to the floor, as shown. I unroll the top a little at a time and smooth the fullness to the outside edges

Foundation Quilting

In order to reduce unnecessary bulk, I trim the batting and backing so that only about 3" remain beyond the quilt top on all sides. As an extra precaution to ensure the quilt layers stay together during the quilting process, I like to do what I call foundation quilting. I use the walking foot to stitch in the ditch in a few key areas. For this quilt, I stitched in the ditch around each concentric row. This allows me to fold the quilt up and move it or store it for an indefinite period of time until I can quilt it. With the spray adhesive and the foundation quilting, I am sure the quilt will stay together.

Thread Tension

Before I begin quilting on the quilt, I like to check the thread tension on a sandwich of scraps. I prepare a sandwich using scraps from my quilt, and then sew using various tension settings.

Since a quilt is bulkier than most other sewing, I often have to increase the thread tension.

If the thread tension is too loose, the top thread will show on the back side of the quilt and the bobbin thread may even lie straight. This occurs when the tension setting is set on too low a number.

If the thread tension is too tight, the bobbin thread will show on the top side of the quilt and may even cause the seam to pucker. This occurs when the tension setting is set on too high a number.

If the thread tension is set correctly, the top and bobbin threads will meet in the middle. This will result in a perfect stitch on both the top and bottom of the quilt.

Stitch Length

Another thing I like to check before I start quilting on my actual quilt is the stitch length. After I have a thread tension I like, I try various stitch lengths to see which one works best for the quilt. Since a quilt is bulkier than most other sewing, I prefer a longer stitch length.

No matter which stitch length I decide on for the quilting, I usually start and end my stitching with a length of nearly nothing and gradually increase to the desired length. This will anchor the thread and is less noticeable than a knot or 'fix' stitch.

Quilting with the Walking Foot (or Dual Feed Foot)

With the proper thread tension and stitch length selected, I am ready to start quilting. I begin by pulling the bobbin thread to the top of the quilt. This is easily done by holding onto the top thread, taking the needle in and out of the fabric, and then pulling the top thread until the bobbin thread loop appears. Pull the loop to bring the full tail of the bobbin thread to the top of the quilt. To begin quilting, hold onto both the top and bobbin thread for the first couple of stitches. (Remember, these first stitches are at a reduced length.) This eliminates the possibility of having a ball of bobbin thread on the backside of the quilt. Pulling the bobbin thread to the top is not as important when you are sewing a regular seam, because the entire seam will be within the quilt. However, every stitch of the quilting will show, and both the top and bottom threads are important. See the following photos.

keeps the sandwich together and even, so one side is not getting ahead of the other. Quilting with the walking foot provides a nice even seam with very little puckering or pulling of the layers.

I like to start in the center of the quilt and work my way outward, stitching the first couple of rows in the ditch. This term means that the quilting will occur in the seam between two pieces of fabric. This method of quilting is very subtle and does not show up much on the front of the quilt once it is completed. However, it does help to secure the layers of the quilt sandwich together.

Since the walking foot only feeds the fabric through the machine in one direction, you will need to turn the entire quilt to change directions. This is why I usually only use the walking foot for my foundation quilting and any long geometric lines that encircle the whole quilt, like in a border.

The first bit of quilting I do on a quilt is a couple of rows using a walking foot. A walking foot is a special foot that helps feed the fabric through the machine from the top. It works in conjunction with the feed dogs which move the fabric through the machine from the bottom. When working with a quilt sandwich, it is very helpful to have the fabric guided through the machine from both the top and bottom. This

Freemotion Quilting

Once I have the quilt layers secure with some foundation quilting, I usually switch to the freemotion foot to do the rest of the quilting. The change to this foot may require an adjustment to the machine settings, including the thread tension. I find that I often have to increase the thread tension when I am freemotion quilting.

Another setting I adjust is to make the machine stop stitching with the needle in the down position. This way when I stop stitching to reposition my hands or the quilt, I can be assured that the stitch is not going anywhere. When I start quilting again, I try to take my first stitch in place. This allows the quilt to release any tension caused by repositioning.

A freemotion foot is a special foot that is used with the feed dogs disengaged. This allows you to guide the quilt, rather than the feed dogs moving the quilt through the machine. The biggest advantage to the freemotion quilting is that you can quilt in any direction, without needing to turn the entire quilt. Simply move the fabric in the direction you want to quilt. I will not only do the free flowing designs with the freemotion foot, but I also use it when I am doing geometric lines, especially if they are in the middle of the quilt. It is so much easier than trying to turn a big quilt through the little opening of the sewing machine.

As a rule of thumb, if you are quilting a random meandering design, do not cross the threads. This will go a long way in preventing the quilt from looking like a big ball of thread. However, when doing a motif or geometric pattern, don't be afraid to double stitch lines. Double stitching a line is preferred to stopping and restarting a line. Not only is it faster, but the thread is more secure. The more often the stitching is started

and stopped, the more chances of the quilting coming undone. Once I realized you could double stitch over portions of the quilting design, I felt like a whole new world of opportunity opened up. Quilting designs that I had thought were only appropriate for hand quilting now became possible for machine quilting. Grid quilting was no longer an endless game of stopping and starting, but became one long continuous line of stitching.

Another important thing to remember when freemotion quilting, is to be very careful to move the top and bottom of the quilt together. This will reduce the chances of puckering on the backside. Adding an extended sewing surface to the machine may help to support more of the quilt and eliminate some of the tension put on the layers, resulting in less puckering. If puckering does occur, I like to remove the stitches causing the puckering and requilt the area. Pressing with steam can sometimes reduce the fullness and help the backing fabric lie flat.

Fab-U-Motion™ fabric mover with Stitch Regulator by Quilter's Cruise Control® is the thing that I found has improved my quilting the most. The fabric mover table is on ball bearings and easily glides in all directions. The stitch regulator helps to keep the stitch length more consistent, the faster you move the table, the faster the needle goes. I move the table and am not tugging on the quilt, so it is much easier to keep the backside lying smoothly.

If the machine has a stitch regulator, that can help keep the stitches even.

Preparing the Quilt for Binding

It is time to prepare for the binding once the entire quilt, with the exception of the last border, is quilted. Place the quilt on a flat surface and cut away the excess on all 4 sides of the quilt. To ensure the border is a consistent width around the entire quilt, use an acrylic ruler to measure a consistent distance from the seam of the last border. With a large cutting mat under the edge of the quilt, cut away the excess as shown.

Preparing the Binding

1. Cut (10) 2½" width of fabric strips from Light fabric #1. Sew the strips together into one continuous strip, using a 45⁰ seam. Start by placing two strips, right sides together, at 90⁰ to each other. Pin them together and draw a 45⁰ line where the strips intersect each other. Sew on the line.

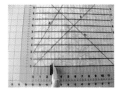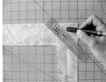

2. Cut ¼" away from the seam. Repeat until all pieces are joined together into one long continuous piece. This 45⁰ angle seam will reduce the bulk of the seam allowance. This will make it easier to sew the binding onto the quilt.

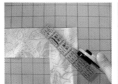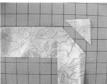

3. Press the seam of each joint, then press the seam allowance open. Fold the binding in half lengthwise with wrong sides together and press.

Attaching the Binding

Before sewing the binding onto the quilt, adjust the needle positioin so it is ¼" away from the inside edge of the walking foot. Leaving a tail of several inches, align the raw edges of the binding with the raw edges of the quilt. Sew together using a ¼" seam allowance and stopping ¼" from the corner of the quilt.

Mitering the Corners of the Binding

Pull the quilt away from the sewing machine. Smooth the binding flat and let it extend beyond the edge of the quilt. Pull the extension up at a

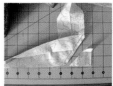

right angle to the edge of the quilt, creating a straight line with the edge of the quilt. Crease the 45º angle created in the binding. Holding that crease in place, fold down the extension of the binding and align with the raw edges of the next side of the quilt. Continue stitching. Repeat with the next 3 corners. Stop sewing several inches from the beginning. Leave a tail of binding.

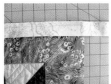

Joining the Ends of the Binding

1. Place 1 tail on top of the other so they overlap. Cut away the excess tails until the overlap is equal to the width of the cut binding (2½").

2. Pull the tails of the binding away from the quilt and place them right sides together, at a 90º angle. Mark the 45º line as shown in the next column. Sew along the drawn line, then cut ¼" from the seam. Unsew some of the binding, if necessary, to get enough room to overlap, mark, and sew. Refold the binding and place against the quilt, aligning the raw edges. Sew the rest of the binding. Press the seam, then press the binding away from the quilt.

Quilting the Last Border

By waiting until the binding is attached to the front of the quilt, it is easier to center the design in the last border. For this quilt, I did a simple design of concentric lines. I used the edge of the walking foot along the binding to get a nice even and consistent spacing. Turning at the corner is easy with the mitered seam. Simply turn the quilt when the mitered seam is reached.

Securing the Binding to the Back Side of the Quilt

Fold the binding to the backside of the quilt, aligning the folded edge with the seam that attached the binding. Use clips to hold the edge in place. Use a blind hemstitch and secure the binding. Tack the mitered flaps in the corners. Wash and dry the quilt, if desired. Add a label on the back.

BUILDING BLOCKS, detail.
Full quilt on page 4.

About the Author

PHOTO: BOB GOSSELIN, WWW.BOBGOSSELINPHOTOGRAPHY.COM

Diane currently resides in Grasonville, Maryland where she moved with her husband after their marriage in 2000. The pair founded their very own landscape architecture consulting firm, Streetscapes, Inc., which they run out of their home.

She became interested in sewing at a very early age, using her mother's scrap fabric to fashion clothes for her dolls before she was even old enough to use a needle. She started sewing clothes for herself when she was about 12 and has not stopped sewing ever since.

She graduated from the Pennsylvania State University with a Bachelor of Science in Landscape Architecture. After college she moved from Pennsylvania to Maryland to start her new job as a landscape architect. With her first paycheck she bought herself a sewing machine. In between making new friends in her new state, Diane sewed outfits for work, home décor pieces, and curtains.

She eventually started quilting after her sisters took a few classes and told her how much fun it was. Her husband shared in her enthusiasm by buying her a new sewing machine just for quilting. He told her it was time to retire her 25 year old machine and get with the times.

Living a state away from her sisters and mom, Diane had to find her own local quilting resources. She began by taking a class at a local quilt shop. From there she was invited to join a quilt group and then went on to join an official quilt guild. She has entered her projects in state and local fairs, as well as participated in a few national competitions.

She was inspired to write this book because she is continually encountering people who are interested in sewing, but cannot find a class or reference book to cover the techniques needed to make their sewing more efficient and accurate.

She still enjoys sewing clothes, home décor projects, and window treatments, but attributes her quilting to her improved precision and accuracy. She continues to be delighted with the dear friends she has come to know through this wonderful craft!

More AQS Books

This is only a small selection of the books available from the American Quilter's Society. AQS books are known worldwide for timely topics, clear writing, beautiful color photos, and accurate illustrations and patterns. The following books are available from your local bookseller, quilt shop, or public library.

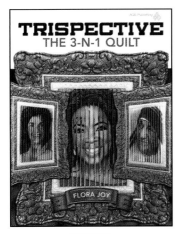

#10281

#10280

#10272

#10283

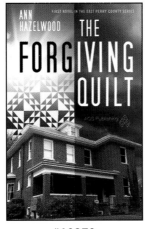

#10279

#10285

#10757

#10275

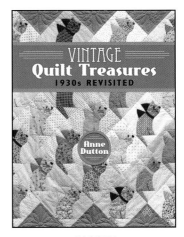

#10277

LOOK for these books nationally.
CALL or VISIT our website at

1-800-626-5420
www.AmericanQuilter.com